"Thy Kingdom Come"
My Life in God's Kingdom

by

Nicholas Fuerst

RoseDog Books

PITTSBURGH, PENNSYLVANIA 15222

RoseDog Books
701 Smithfield Street
Pittsburgh, PA 15222
Visit our website at *www.rosedogbookstore.com*

ISBN: 978-1-4349-8435-7
eISBN: 978-1-4349-7426-6

"Thy Kingdom Come"

My Life in God's Kingdom

by

Nicholas Fuerst

Dedication

To all those who have had any part in my recognizing God's Kingdom—
God's blessings and my thanks.

For all those who, living in God's Kingdom, have yet to recognize it—
God's blessings and my prayers.

Acknowledgements

Reverend Joseph Kleppner – Pastor,
St. Frances Cabrini Parish, Aliquippa, PA.—
theological proofreading and advisement.

Julie and Michael Fuerst – daughter-in-law
and son — transcription and technical assistance.

Patty Fuerst-my wife and best friend forever—
without whom I would not be who I am.

Any monies received by the author from the publication of this book will be donated to support world wide disaster relief efforts.

Table of Contents

Introduction

Whenever I start reading a new book, I feel a sense of anticipation and excitement. I have high hopes and expectations that the author will be transmitting new ideas and concepts that will educate, inspire, and motivate me, and somehow make my life better.

As I write these lines, I am hoping that you, the reader, will be in a similar frame of mind. Perhaps the ideas and concepts I'm presenting will indeed be educational, inspirational, and motivational for you. By the time you reach the "Conclusion," I hope your life will be better.

If you believe in God, please keep reading. And if by chance you don't believe in God, you are certainly welcome to continue on as well. What I am going to say here is especially meant for anyone who can sincerely say, "I believe in God." It is meant for those who somehow know, deep in their hearts, that there is an incomprehensible being that has created all that exists, maintains all that exists, and even in time, reclaims all who proclaim him as Lord of their lives. Those who believe that God exists would likely agree that they believe so because the great preponderance of information and experiences in their lives has convinced them of this experienced-but-unseen reality.

As much as it is in the minds and desires of mankind to define and possess God, it is not possible. God is simply not fully knowable here and now. What little we think we do know about God melts into the admission that God is, this side of Heaven, unknowable. As people of Godly faith we can only know that He exists. Beyond that, we must admit that God is a mystery despite all the wonders and complexities of the human mind that come to bear on this issue. Man as far as we can tell, is the pinnacle and most significant of God's creations, save the angels themselves. But that's only our opinion as we observe who we are from our own perspective. Maybe our God of indescribable and unknowable greatness has created even more superior beings than ourselves in other realms. Regardless, the point is that in this realm and from our perspective we can know that God exists, but much beyond that we can only have hopeful thinking and faith.

I'm a Catholic. I always have been, and expect I always will be. My Catholic Christian faith is the most precious gift I've ever received. I am totally convinced that my faith is even more important than the gift of life itself. I perceive that my life without this faith and its coincident promises, especially including eternal life, would hold no apparent or significant value. The strength of my faith and the mechanisms of my religion have allowed me to cope with every challenge I've ever encountered. If you are Catholic, my hope for this book is that you will be somehow reinforced and energized, and may even become more dedicated to living out your Catholic Christian challenge. If you are not Catholic, my hope for this book is that you will take heart that Godly living is a reward in and of itself, and also has rewards beyond this life which your dedicated and committed faith essentially guarantees.

The spiritual reality that God is in my life has, since even my youngest years and earliest recollections, been the highest priority in my life. By frequent and focused connecting with God through the sacraments, Mass, and prayer, I now maintain a nearly continuous, conscious awareness of God. My thoughts flow repeatedly and frequently over the questions of, "What does God want me to do?" and "What is His will for me?" I feel very much aware that everything that touches my life, from the simple drawing of a breath, to suffering a physical pain, to enjoying a worldly pleasure, to contemplating the vagaries of the future, and so on, yes everything is overtly connected to God. Everything, in that sense, has for me become holy. Everything is in, and of God's realm. It is with this realization that living in God's Kingdom even within the limits of time and space, has become a reality for me. This approach to life—the seeking out, and the living out of God's will, puts me in a constant state of mind and spirit that I've come to understand as living in God's Kingdom here on Earth.

In these pages I have taken to trying to articulate this wonderful awareness that allows me to live in the earthly realm of God, like those in the heavenly realm—without fear, and without anxiety, and where even my sufferings have redemptive value. Living in this state has generated within me a deep and compelling desire and need to share these concepts with others, so that they too may live their lives confidently and joyfully in the presence of God's great works and great promises. As I present the materials herein, I often use the terms "we", and "us". I do so, not because I can say that I know, or think that I know, that these concepts and experiences apply to everyone, but rather it is because I am hopeful that other believers might also come to the awareness of the promising and fulfilling nature of living in God's earthly Kingdom as I believe I have.

An accurate bibliography for the materials included in this book is not really possible since the ideas and concepts presented are the conglomeration of many different readings and experiences over the course of most of my lifetime. I have included a listing of "Resources" at the end that have contributed to my knowledge, awareness and convictions, and which may be helpful to the reader wishing to further his own awareness of Kingdom thinking and living.

Chapter 1: Who Am I to be Speaking About God's Kingdom?

I was born the third of six children to Catholic parents of modest means in the mid twentieth century. Mom and Dad were both dedicated throughout their lives to the Catholic way of life. I, like my three brothers and two sisters, was raised Catholic and was expected to receive the initiating sacraments of the Catholic Church, to attend Mass on Sundays and Holy Days, and to receive religious instructions from grade school through high school. In the process of all that, with my bashful and introverted personality as it was, I developed a somewhat scrupulous conscience, and perhaps a greater than necessary sense of guilt for my transgressions and misgivings. But at the same time I unwittingly nurtured a healthy sense of respect for my elders and superiors, as well as for my peers. Toward God, I felt awe and holy fear, and a love for the Almighty. I had a certainty that I was loved unconditionally by Him. I also "got" the connection that whatever I did to please my parents was pleasing to God, and whatever I did to please God was pleasing to my parents. So, early on in my life, I was developing at least a rudimentary awareness of God's presence — both afar in Heaven, as well as in my own life.

Being the reserved personality that I was, and being anxious and fearful of the unknown and the as yet unfamiliar world around me, I often found myself consciously accepting, tolerating, and holding in negative feelings. Whenever I was verbally or emotionally affronted, I gladly resorted to the traditional Catholic lesson of "offering it up" — asking God to use my sufferings, as small as they might be, to create goodness somewhere in the world.

As a bewildered high school kid, I experienced frequently and confidently the feeling that I was somewhat like a rose bud, being a wonderful creation of God, but not yet being complete, and therefore destined to develop, and "blossom" into something much more profoundly significant. I, of course, had no idea how or when that might happen, but by virtue of my faith and sense of hope, I took comfort that God's will and plans would eventually bring me to that point. I frequently prayed that God would not only reveal His will for me, but also that He would give me the necessary strength to embrace it and to live it out in my life. I wanted God to use me for His purposes. I distinctly recall being aware of, and repeating frequently to myself, the lines from the prophet Isaiah,

"Then I heard the voice of the Lord saying, 'Whom shall I send? Who will go for us?' 'Here I am' I said, 'Send me!'" (Isaiah 6:8).

Even at that time in my life, and in significant ways I was connecting things in this life with things of God.

When I went off to college, I was very fearful of what I had been told happened to many college students — that they "lost their faith." I had no idea how that could happen, and I also knew that I loved my faith and that I didn't want to trade it for a college degree. With the anticipation that college courses would be so much more difficult than high school courses, I immersed myself promptly and deeply into my studies, but I also consciously attended to my spiritual and religious life. I made sure to pray privately each and every day. I attended Mass for sure on Sundays and Holy Days, and very often on week days as well. I also made sure to receive the sacraments of Reconciliation and Eucharist frequently. It didn't take very long in my freshman year to realize, on that Catholic campus, that those students who were losing their faith weren't somehow having it fiendishly wrested from them, but rather they themselves were making decisions to *not* practice their religion and to *not* do the things that had nurtured and sustained their faith up until that time. Their faith and the direction it could have led them, had they chosen to invest themselves in it, was shrinking, and ebbing away from them. For me, the college years, despite excruciating academic pressures, were also years of tenacious efforts to maintain and mature my faith. It has since become clear to me that without my college challenges, I would certainly have been excluded from the career that I have been so blessed with and that I treasure so dearly. I would also have been excluded from this particular ministry to God's people. I likely would also not have developed the spiritual sense of conviction and purpose that I now have.

Being of firm awareness and conviction that my vocation, my calling in life, was like Jesus Himself, service to God and service to others, I made conscious attempts to participate in service projects and organizations in my high school, college, and medical school years. I can distinctly recall feeling very uneasy with those efforts, as they were mostly contrived, awkward, and even at times insincere. I often didn't feel what I thought I should have been feeling with such efforts, namely, self fulfillment, worthiness, or goodness. But I kept seeking out and participating in such activities, knowing that Jesus Christ Himself had come "not to be served but to serve" (Matthew 20:28).

I had real life models and heroes in my background that convinced me also that service to others was "the way to go" and could really become a way of life. I had my childhood pediatrician, Dr. Thomas Benson. There was a missionary doctor to Southeast Asia, Dr. Tom Dooley. And there was a missionary doctor to Africa, Dr. Albert Schweitzer. It was Albert Schweitzer who commented to a college graduating class, "I don't know what your destiny will be, but one thing I know, the only ones among you who will be truly happy are those who will seek and find how to serve." Again, I was finding things of this earthly realm connecting with things of God and His heavenly realm. And so I continued my efforts at service, hopeful that God would use them for His purposes.

During my late high school years I discovered and read a book that I took to college with me, and re-read countless times. It was entitled The Meaning of Success by Michel Quoist (see "Resources"-A.37). To this day, I know that the concepts I extracted from that book have formed me and affected the pursuit of my vocation more than any other single book I've ever read. It presented not only the same solid Christian philosophy that I had always held and espoused, but also presented real and concrete ways to live it out in daily life. It addressed all the issues of love — love of self, love of others, and love of God. These concepts allowed my puny, anemic efforts at service to take on a vibrant spiritual significance despite the often empty inner personal feelings that accompanied them. It was in this book that I came across what I now consider to be the key to living in the Kingdom during our worldly lives. Quoist wrote, "If you want to be free, young in spirit, joyous, peaceful, strong, and successful each day, each minute, "Cast thy cares upon the Lord and He will sustain thee." (Psalm 54:23).As I consciously integrated this concept into my daily life, even as a student, I realized that I was only human, and could handle only so much. I found worries, anxieties, negative emotions, anger, and resentment could all be dismissed and heaped onto the strength of God who was the highest priority in my life. Any possibility of loss, failure, and even death, was not an issue as I grew in the conviction that God's will for me in my life would occur, only if I didn't resist. I accepted whatever occurred in my life and gave thanks to God for it, because I knew by faith that it was God's will for me. Many of the occurrences back then that I thought were negative, have in retrospect turned out to be formative and even pivotal experiences that have pushed me along the path to where I am today — a strong and confident God- centered life with the conviction that He will always be with me and will guide me to where He wants me to be.

In college I discovered the "Sermon on the Mount" (Matthew 5:12-7:29). I read it over and over again, contemplating and trying to discover the true meaning of its lines and how it should apply to me. I remember especially pondering and being puzzled by the listing of the "Beatitudes" (see "Resources"-C.3). I was aware by that time in my life that riches and earthly gains were not worthwhile goals for my limited time on the face of this earth. The more I considered the statements of the beatitudes (literally, "the blessings"), the more it really did make sense that my life could be very much fulfilled by being "poor in spirit," "meek," "merciful," "clean of heart," and by being a "peacemaker." Each of the beatitudes identifies us with Christ, but the final one lets us know that we should expect to be insulted, persecuted, and slandered if we truly wish to identify with and be close to Christ. In these situations, we are told to "rejoice and be glad for your reward will be great in heaven." And we are again reminded of our need to expect suffering and sacrifice in our lives when later in the Gospel of Matthew, Jesus says,

"Whoever does not take up his cross and follow after me is not worthy of me. Whoever finds his life will lose it, and whoever loses his life for my sake will find it." (Matthew 10:38-39).

I also discovered the "Prayer of St. Francis of Assisi," and committed it to memory. I repeated it thoughtfully day in and day out begging God to choose me as His servant in bringing true peace to others:

> Lord, make me an instrument of thy peace;
> where there is hatred let me sow love;
> where there is injury, pardon;
> where there is doubt, faith;
> where there is despair, hope;
> where there is darkness, light;
> and where there is sadness, joy.
> O, Divine Master, grant that I may not so much seek
> to be consoled, as to console;
> to be understood, as to understand;
> to be loved, as to love.
> For, it is in giving that we receive,
> in pardoning that we are pardoned,
> and in dying that we are born into eternal life. Amen.

I began to sense how I needed always and everywhere to be open to God's will, and to be ready to do His work in this world, for the sake of attaining the eternal heavenly reward for myself and with others. I became aware that in giving of myself, without the expectations of being paid back, I would be showing God's love to others, and thereby would be bringing His peace into their lives. I was quite satisfied to think that this was a big part of what God wanted and expected from me. Once again the connection between Heaven and Earth, the seen and the unseen, was becoming apparent to me.

As I proceeded through the balance of my formal education and training, I continued purposely and purposefully to maintain contact with the spiritual and religious modalities that had brought me to that point — reading, reflection, prayer, Mass, and the sacraments. Quite unexpectedly, and not as part of any plans that I had made, I met and started dating my wife-to-be, Patty. In addition to being a true friend and wonderful companion, she brought good things to my life that I had never experienced prior to that time. There was humor, and a sense of human love and caring unlike any I had ever experienced before. I had an awareness of not only being accepted by another person, but actually being desired by her. The comfort, calmness, and warmth I felt and saw in that relationship seemed very right for me, and in the context of my life up until that time, it felt very holy. After much discernment, the confident reception of the sacrament of Matrimony ensued. This sacrament, this covenant commitment, has been the conscious focus of my daily life ever since — and that's well over thirty years now. Hardly a day has gone by that I haven't marveled at what a wonderful part of the earthly Kingdom of God occurs through the sacrament of Matrimony. In recent years, at my son's wedding, the priest's homily included a profound statement about married love. He said, "It's not so much love that sustains the marriage, as it is marriage that sustains the love." This also brings to mind the connection between God's heavenly Kingdom in the goodness of the sacraments, and God's earthly Kingdom in the goodness of human love.

So who am I to be speaking about God's Kingdom? Please be clear about who I am not. I am not an authority in any sense, and I have no "degree." I'm not a clergyman. I'm not a theologian or a scripture scholar. I'm not a person of unique or unusual capabilities. I'm not even a person with some "outside the box" approach to life. Who I am is a person who has been blessed with certain privileges in this life. By the grace of God I have a devoted and long enduring family that has been encouraging and supportive of me. I'm a physician who finds daily satisfaction, fulfillment, and holiness in my work and in the people (patients, staff, and colleagues) I work with and for. I'm a person who has found, though never consciously searched for, financial security, and makes purposeful efforts to share what I have with others. I'm a layman who treasures his faith and religion to the utmost, and I have chosen to invest myself in those issues that absolutely matter and make a difference. I'm a man who has become confident that in living in this life with God and His work as my highest priority always and everywhere, I can eventually attain everlasting life in God's Kingdom of Heaven. And as for the here and now, as this book declares, I am a man who has discovered the earthly Kingdom of God and has chosen to live in it until the heavenly Kingdom becomes available to me.

So, if I have any qualification to speak about the Kingdom of God, it is by merit of my being, like all of us, a creation of God. Beyond that, being baptized into the life of Christ, I am a child of God who has become immersed in the responsibilities that are at the center of that commitment. As such, I have the desire and responsibility to share with others the good news that I have been so privileged to discover in the course of living my life in the presence of God. Because of this awareness, I feel a great need, and a strong responsibility to articulate this which seems most amazing to me. Something maybe others haven't experienced, or if they have, maybe they need to have their feelings or experiences corroborated. Or maybe someone who never had this thought before will think it for the first time. Or maybe someone who is on the brink of discovering this breakthrough way of thinking and living will actually break through, and thereby have their lives transformed favorably, and in holy ways.

I've been aware for many years now that not only is living in the Kingdom in this earthly realm a possibility, but it can be a reality. I've been enjoying this spiritual way of life personally, and feeling quite gifted and blessed by it. I've had the thought that if all mankind were aware of, and willing to live this way, we would have almost literally "Heaven on Earth." There would be no need for borders or selfishness; no need for killing or stealing. There would be no evil, only goodness; no wars, only peace; no fighting, only cooperation; no anger or grudges, only mercy and forgiveness; no hatred, only love. There would be nothing but goodness, and nothing but Godliness. Now really, isn't that our concept of the heavenly Kingdom? That state of being in which only peace, love, comfort, security, goodness and Godliness exist? Amen!!!

Chapter 2: Identifying the Kingdom of God

What is the Kingdom of God

A kingdom is a ruling system in which the king has the ultimate authority over, and responsibility for, a territory and its population. We say that the designated territory and people are the king's realm, and his domain. If we should speak in the spiritual terms of God's Kingdom, then we are referring to God as the King, the one who has the ultimate authority over and responsibility for the entire realm, which of course we also attribute to Him as being the creator of. Said another way, all that is relevant to God, which is everything that exists (because He has created all), is God's Kingdom. Our Christian creeds (see "Resources"-B.12) use the terms "heaven and earth," and "all that is seen and unseen," as being the creations of God. So in that sense we might say that God's Kingdom consists of the universe and beyond — things we can understand and things we can't understand. We have to think that truly there are many phenomena "out there" that we cannot even conceive of. Although we may feel comfortable in our knowable earthly realm, there is so much that is unknown, and so much that is mystery that surrounds us. This should not frighten us or make us feel insecure, but rather should allow us to sense that God exists, and beyond that should prod us to search for Him throughout our lifetimes.

We who populate this earthly realm of His Kingdom are His subjects. He provides for all of our needs, and yet gives us free choice in how we decide to respond to Him. In return for His care, He deserves our never ending allegiance and obedience. We should always be listening for His invitations, and be ready to respond to them. As Christians, we realize that God our King, in all His goodness, does not rule from afar, or in silence. He actually has been, continues to be, and has promised that He always will be with us here in this world as well as in eternity. We know from the Hebrew Scriptures (the Old Testament) that God was present to His people through the prophets and the covenants. And we know from the Christian scriptures (the New Testament) that God incarnated Himself in the man named Jesus of Nazareth, who became Jesus the Christ. So, as we come to know Jesus by His life and words, as we discover them in the Christian scriptures, so we come to know God and His plans for us. St. Paul wrote, "Christ Jesus is the image of the invisible God" (Colossians 1:15).

Even as limited beings living in a limited realm, we can realize that whatever is objectively seemingly knowable and able to be experienced began with and belongs to God. As such, those things are part of His Kingdom — but only part of it. Therefore whatever we know or experience within the confines of our earthly lives can certainly be referred to as God's Kingdom on Earth. In a similar and parallel manner, we anticipate by faith that all that exists in God's heavenly realm is also of His Kingdom. In that heavenly state of existence, the angels and saints do His bidding willingly and perfectly, and sing His praises joyfully and unceasingly while fully in His presence, in His perfection, and in His love, on into eternity.

For us to recognize God as our King while we are still in this earthly realm is an amazing discovery. It leads us to a here and now existence of security, peace, hope, confidence, and even faith centered certainty. By living in the confines of this world as "good and faithful servant(s)" (Matthew 25:21) of God our King, we are clearly preparing for our eventual transformation and entrance into God's eternal Kingdom of Heaven.

Where is the Kingdom of God?

The Kingdom of God, as far as our limited human minds can perceive, exists in two portions. The one which we may most commonly think of is the heavenly Kingdom. In this realm, only spirits can exist — God Himself of course, the angels, and the saints. The saints are those human beings who have lived Godly lives, shed their bodies in death, and been transformed to immortality whereby they can see God face to face and exist in his presence eternally. But the point of these writings is to focus on what we can know and experience while we are here in this life, and in this world. And that is what we can refer to as the earthly Kingdom of God.

As much as we can bring our minds to focus on things of God, we can say that the Kingdom of God really does exist and that, at least in part, it exists right here surrounding us on all sides. As we experience God's creations, and as we experience things of God, we are experiencing the earthly Kingdom of God. Here in this realm, God's Kingdom includes the trees and grass; the stars and sun and moon; the rain and snow; the hail and wind; these people and that race; that land and those oceans. God's reality and His existence can be recognized in His creations — in this tree right here in front of me; in me, and in this person right here next to me; in that star millions of light years away, and in every atom between here and there. So in this way we can know that God really does exist with us here on Earth, right here and right now. And once time and space and our planet exist no more, the reality that all things have come from God will be obviously clear and eternally evident.

Whatever God has created, which of course is everything, and wherever God exists, which of course is everywhere, is His realm, His Kingdom. That being said, it becomes obvious that the Kingdom really is present right here. It is only necessary for us to recognize it as such, to accept it as such, and then to live in it as such, by living holy lives. By making Godly things the center of our lives, we are living worthily in His Kingdom on Earth. By doing so, we are also preparing ourselves to be worthy of, and some day capable of, being transformed from worldly mortal existences into heavenly immortal existences.

The Kingdom on Earth can be defined in part by the limits of time and space. But the Kingdom in Heaven is not limited by time and space, and therefore rightly should not be referred to as a place. We often speak about people dying and "going to Heaven," suggesting that they are, in some way, packing up and heading to another destination. This might be a simple and pleasant concept, but one which leaves us still thinking in terms of time and space. The heavenly Kingdom, the eternal, timeless Kingdom hereafter, perhaps should not be thought of as a place, but rather as a state of the soul's existence. Perhaps we should abandon those concepts of our eternal destiny, be it known as Heaven or Hell, as being "up there" or "down there," or as the "pearly gates," or the "fires of hell." More appropriately, Heaven can be expected to be the soul's ecstatic joy at its presence before, and its union with, God eternally, while Hell can be expected to be the soul's horrible agony and sorrow at its separation from God eternally.

Why Should We Live in the Kingdom of God?

Yes! Indeed! Why should we live in the Kingdom? More importantly, why should we *want* to live in the Kingdom? The reason is because, as it is, we really have no choice. This earthly realm is God's Kingdom whether we recognize it or not, whether we like it or not, and whether we choose to accept it as such or not. We can't change that! To me, it's like the Mack truck barreling down the street. The reality of that truck and its potential deadly effect on me is the same whether I choose to believe in it or not. If I believe that it is real and step out in front of it, I will be killed. If I don't believe that it is real, and step out in front of it, I will, likewise, be killed. So the reality is the same whether I believe it or not. Similarly, since we have no choice but to live in this earthly realm, right here and now, it is only a matter of whether we recognize it as being a portion of God's Kingdom or not. My awareness has become, and the reality that I am personally convinced of and living according to, is that this life is part of God's Kingdom. And I am absolutely convinced that if others do likewise, they also will be living a hopeful and inspired existence presently, while preparing for the inevitability of God's heavenly Kingdom in eternity.

With that being said, we come back to the question of why should we *want* to live, in this life, honoring God as our King, and living in His domain? The reason of course is because to ignore God is to ignore all that is good. It is to ignore all the possibilities for love, comfort, and security that only the King can provide for us. And most importantly, the failure to recognize our place and situation as being governed by God as King, is to accept a life time of uncertainty as to what our ultimate status will be in the hereafter. To refuse the Kingdom in this realm, is to refuse the Kingdom in the next realm as well, for God is the King of both. God is the King of all! Conversely, to accept the Kingdom in this realm is to prepare for, and to accept, the Kingdom in the next realm. The only difference between the two portions of His Kingdom is that our souls are encumbered with bodies in this realm, whereas they are isolated spirits in the next.

So really there is no rational reason that I can discern, given the above awareness, not to take God and His Kingdom work seriously, and to accept it willingly, and even joyfully, so that one day the King will welcome us into His heavenly Kingdom as "good and faithful servant(s)"(Matthew 25:21).

In the Christian faith we believe that God-seeking people who have died and left this realm of earthly existence enter into a presently invisible and un-knowable realm that we call eternity, which is not bound by time or space. We believe that those who have led Godly lives of the nature described in the Christian scriptures, will enter into His presence in the eternal Kingdom that we call Heaven. We also believe that those who have denied God in this life will be banished from His presence eternally, which we call Hell. And those who for whatever reason have not had the opportunity to encounter God in this life, we can confidently entrust their souls and their eternity to His endless love and mercy.

Right here and now, we can certainly recall those who have passed on before us to that wonderful destiny of heavenly eternity. We can recall when they were here, present with us. We should not, and need not, feel separated from them. We should simply feel a different kind of connection with them. This is what we as Christians refer to as "the Communion of Saints." It is a reality of our faith that the souls, presently existing in the earthly Kingdom, are truly in communication with the souls now existing in the heavenly Kingdom. Those of us in the earthly realm cannot experience, because of the limits of time and space and our physical nature, the realities of those existing in the heavenly realm. We can only contemplate and spiritually feel the con-nection. Those in the heavenly realm exist knowing and having experienced what we in this earthly realm are experiencing, but also knowing and expe-riencing what the eternal, heavenly Kingdom is about. They have that state of being and knowledge for eternity. We in the earthly realm can only be envious of those in the heavenly realm because they see God face to face. They have come into that portion of God's Kingdom wherein God becomes completely, and clearly known to them, while in this portion of the Kingdom, the earthly Kingdom, we can only "see" God vaguely by the "eyes" of our faith. By consciously and constantly keeping God in our thoughts, words, and deeds, we can hope for and anticipate that point in time in which our own faithful lives and the faithful lives of our loved ones and the lives of our fellow faithful human beings will be transformed from our earthly mortal forms into our heavenly immortal forms. We should be joyfully anticipating in this life our entrance into the Kingdom in its even better form, in fact in its best form — that of the eternal Kingdom of Heaven.

In this context then, why should we as humans ever be so insecure as to look at our earthly, biologic lives as being so important that we would do almost anything to maintain them when all scientific and circumstantial information lets us know, and leads us to understand, that life as we know it is ebbing away? Said another way, God is always calling us home to that most excellent state of life in His heavenly Kingdom. Why should we worry about trying to maintain our earthly lives beyond a reasonable period of time? The transformation will come sooner or later whether we desire it or not. The point is, God desires it! We know these things by merit of the fact that every human being who has ever lived (with the obvious exception of those of us living now), has died. And so we, the living, can know that as sure as we were born, we also will die. None of us will live in this realm forever. Even if we should somehow eke out another day or two, week or two, or even a year or two, once all is said and done, we will still die and then what difference has it really made? For all our anxiety and effort and maybe even suffering, what have we really gained? There's a euphemism I've heard, that applies to how we should focus on our lives and our goals: "Life is short; eternity is long." Think about it — a hundred years from now (less than a drop in the ocean of time), who will remember or even care that you or I ever lived at all? As far as I can tell, unless we should become canonized saints or other "famous" people, probably no one, with the only significant exception of the One who cared enough to create us in the first place. And at that point of course, we will have been transformed into eternity, and hopefully into His presence which was our heart-and-soul's desire all along anyway. Then we will be dwelling in eternal bliss as we perform His will perfectly, and praise and glorify Him endlessly in the heavenly Kingdom.

> "Therefore I tell you, do not worry about your life. Can any of you by worrying add a single moment to your life span? Why are you anxious? So do not worry and say, 'What are we to eat?' or 'What are we to drink?' or 'What are we to wear?' Your heavenly father knows that you need them all. But seek first the Kingdom of God and His righteousness, and all these things will be given you besides. Do not worry about tomorrow; tomorrow will take care of itself." Matthew 7:25-34.

Certainly in this life, we need to realize therefore that life itself is God's creation, and His gift to us. So too are time and space. And just as with any gift, we honor and please the giver by returning thanks to him for it, and by using the gift in ways it was meant to be used. So, while in this realm of the Kingdom, we must protect and use appropriately our lives, our minds, our talents, our time, and our riches for His purposes, knowing that He wishes to bring us back to His company eventually in the Kingdom of Heaven. And we must be prepared to come into His presence some day with the fruits of the gifts He's given us— the fruits of our worldly endeavors. To remind myself of the need to be diligent and tenacious in His service, I often recite the "Prayer of St. Ignatius Loyola":

"Dearest Lord, teach me to be generous,
Teach me to serve You as You deserve—
to give and not to count the cost,
to fight and not to heed the wounds,
to toil and not to seek for rest,
to labor and not to ask for reward,
save that of knowing I am doing Your will. Amen."

By living in these ways, we will be worthy, as best a worldly creature can be worthy, of entering that Kingdom — the heavenly Kingdom of God, the Kingdom of unimaginable beauty, happiness, and contentment.

"...eye has not seen, and ear has not heard what God has prepared for those who love Him." (Corinthians 2-9).

Who Can Live in the Kingdom of God?

In the Catholic Christian tradition, at the beginning of each Lenten season, on Ash Wednesday, the priest blesses us with ashes on our foreheads, and says the words, "Remember Man, that you are [from] dust, and unto dust you shall return." With this blessing we are reminded before our annual forty day season of prayer, self-denial, and almsgiving, to live our lives humbly. It causes us to pause and remind ourselves that we as individuals, and even as the entire human race, are really not a big deal, or at least we shouldn't be thinking that we are. We, like dust, are quite insignificant. We were created by God's plans and wishes, not by ours. We were created for His purposes, not for ours. Our value is only what God makes it to be, not what we make it to be or think it to be. Our lives are short as measured by time, but never- ending in the eternity that awaits us, and to which we will arrive in the very near future.

So, with that reminder, who are we to be granted the possibility of sharing God's Kingdom here on Earth? We are God's creations. We ourselves are next to nothing, but being that we are from God, our task once we have discovered

God's existence and His presence in our lives, is to search out and discover what He expects of us while we are here in His earthly Kingdom. To discover His will for us is to discover "the narrow gate" that leads to His heavenly Kingdom.

> "Enter through the narrow gate, for the gate is wide and the road broad that leads to destruction, and those who enter through it are many. How narrow the gate and constricted the road that leads to life. And those who find it are few." (Matthew 7: 13-14).

I once heard a saying (its source and author are unknown to me), which is a bit simple, and yet a bit profound. "Life is a game, the object of which is to discover the object of the game." God invites us to know Him by showing us a little bit about Himself in the people, things, and situations that He chooses, by His will alone, to lay before us throughout our lives. It is up to us to recognize through these manifestations, that He is behind it all. And if one realizes that God exists in such ways in his life in this world, then he is blessed with the privilege of living in the Kingdom right here and now. He has a certain secure knowledge by his faith in God's works, that he indeed is included in the realm and the protection of the King. And this is the best we can attain in this earthly realm. But that's plenty good enough, because it allows us as mortals to live holy lives, in humility, in His earthly Kingdom, while we enthusiastically and joyfully anticipate the eventual transformation to the immortality of His overabundant and eternal heavenly Kingdom.

So as far as who can live in God's earthly Kingdom, the answer is obvious. Anyone can! Everyone can! We were all created by Him. We were all placed in this realm of His Kingdom strictly by His plans and for His purposes. If we hear His call and search for Him in this life, and strive to know Him, and to serve Him in this world, we can be assured that we are presently living in His Kingdom and that we will eventually be rewarded with the eternal happiness He has promised us, through the saving work of Jesus Christ.

Chapter 3: Living in the Kingdom of God

The Will of God

Once we have recognized that the Kingdom of God exists in this world, how do we actually go about living in it? Most importantly, we must trust in God as our King to provide all that we need, always and in every situation. We must also accept that God's plans for us are not always our plans for ourselves. And we must commit ourselves to the awareness that His will is what we must do in all situations.

In the course of His living as a man in this world, and revealing the true nature of God to us — Father, Son, and Holy Spirit — Jesus instructed His disciples,

> "This is how you are to pray: Our Father, who are in heaven, hallowed be thy name. Thy Kingdom come. Thy will be done on earth as it is in heaven." (Matthew 6: 9-10).

From this prayer, we can decipher that God's Kingdom does indeed exist in Heaven, and that His Kingdom exists and is available to us here on Earth if we are diligent in doing his will. In praying this way, we can realize and accept God's fatherhood. He is the One who creates, the One who cares, the One who loves, and the One who has ongoing concerns for His creations. "The Lord's Prayer" also instructs us that we can rely on the Father for our needs:

> "Give us today our daily bread, and forgive us our debts as we forgive our debtors, and do not subject us to the final test, but deliver us from the evil one." (Matthew 6: 11-13).

But note well, in addressing our Father in the heavenly realm, we are requesting that His "Kingdom come" to us, meaning here in this earthly realm. We are not requesting that we go to His heavenly realm (although certainly we do hope eventually to do so) but rather that His "Kingdom come" to us — that is, here and now. The prayer says simply but emphatically that we actually already know how that Kingdom can come to us — by doing God's will. "Thy will be done, on earth as it is in heaven." As simple and straight forward as this is stated, actually doing God's will, thereby bringing God's Kingdom into the world, and living in it here and now may not be all that easy because we need to do God's will "as it is [done] in Heaven." That is our divine calling, and our mission here on earth, to make our best and most sincere attempts to search for and to discover God's will for us, and then to carry it out to perfection. Perfection is the way His will is done in heaven, which is that state of awareness and experience of God that makes everything about Him crystal clear. Here in this earthly realm of God's Kingdom, doing anything to perfection is quite impossible. But Jesus teaches us,

> "You...are to be perfect even as your heavenly Father is perfect" (Matthew 5:48).

This is not to say that there might be dire consequences if we don't end up with perfection during the course of our lives here in this world, but rather it is to say that our destiny is to eventually become perfect as we make our best efforts to be holy, Godly people within our capabilities, with the gifts He has given us. We should be trying continuously to approach perfection, to approach God. Perfection is what we will attain when we are transformed from His Kingdom on Earth to His Kingdom in Heaven. This is a very sobering, and yet transcendent thought.

But what if we fall short? What if we miss the calling, the assignment, the real will of God for us? What if our efforts and diligence in the course of our lifetimes have not been as successful as they could have been and should have been? Are we in the end subject to being judged by God as not being worthy to be transformed to His eternal Kingdom? Are we doomed to eternal damnation? The best I can tell based on my experiences of the Kingdom in this world and on my growing faith in God and His loving fatherhood, the answer to this question is, "Certainly not." In fact, "Absolutely not!" God's fatherhood, we know by faith is forever and always merciful. He sees the depths of the hearts of His children. He knows their true desires. He knows their sincerity (or lack thereof) of mind and purpose. He accepts the intents and attempts of those who wish to be in one accord with Him, both here and now, as well as forever in heavenly eternity. At the end of our limited worldly existences, the transformation to eternal life will be rewarded or punished in accordance with the sincerity of our efforts toward Godliness in this realm, not in accordance with the amount of success we've had. Our eternity will be peaceful in accordance with our internal longings and our external efforts regarding the Godly characteristics of love, mercy, and peace in this world. Our eternity will be happy and joyous in accordance with our commitment to exemplify His goodness and joy in this world. Our eternity will be free of fear and anxiety and pain in accordance with our efforts to rid ourselves, and hopefully others, of evil.

Mother Theresa of Calcutta, India said it so simply and so clearly when she encountered a certain news reporter. She was asked how she could feel any real degree of success in her efforts to care for the poorest of the poor in the city streets when there were so many who needed care, and she was providing care to so relatively few. Her response was, "God's work is success. My work is fidelity." So too it is for us. If we stay faithful to our calling to seek God's will for us, and to carry it out to the best of our ability, using the gifts God gave us, He will take care of the rest, causing His will to materialize.

In a recorded retreat that I've listened to many times, entitled, "Behold the Lamb," Reverend Emmanuel Charles McCarthy in discussing how we can bring God's peace to the world, points out that as we choose the means of our living, so will we achieve our end results. Said another way, as we sow, so shall we reap. He uses the example of a farmer sowing seeds. If wheat seeds are sown, the farmer doesn't expect to reap corn. He expects, in fact he knows, he will reap wheat. So too in the spiritual life, if we sow evil, we cannot expect to reap good. If we sow war, we cannot expect to reap peace. If we sow hatred, we cannot expect to reap love. So as we live our lives, we need to live the means now that will achieve the ends we desire. As we choose our means so are we choosing our end results. If we wish to reap peace, "as it is in heaven," we must sow peace here and now. If we wish to reap love and goodness, "as it is in heaven," we must sow love and goodness here and now. If we wish to reap mercy and forgiveness, "as it is in heaven," we must sow mercy and forgiveness here and now. If we are to reap Godliness, we must sow Godliness here and now. Nothing less should be expected by those who wish to live in God's Kingdom here on Earth, as well as in Heaven. As St. Paul wrote,

> "Do not be deceived: God cannot be mocked. A man reaps what he sows. The one who sows to please his sinful nature...will reap destruction." (Galatians 6:7-8).

Our mortality, as sure as anything can be sure, will be transformed to immortality sooner or later. It becomes very urgent therefore to search for, to discover, and to carry out God's will if we are to reap the rewards that He offers and that our hearts so dearly desire.

For me, one of the best and ongoing ways I have of consciously reminding myself of these characteristics of our merciful and caring God, is to say the "Prayer of St. Francis" (see "Resources" - B.1) at the beginning of each day. I do this as soon as I get in my car and head off to work. I say the prayer slowly, and thoughtfully, focusing on the true meaning of each phrase, and consider its implications for how I will live out this particular day. I consider my work to be not so much how I make a living as it is how I serve God by ministering to His people. The "Prayer of St. Francis" helps me to focus on serving others by conveying to them the goodness of God. When I'm in the work place, I consciously recall that I am to be like Jesus would be in all that I think and do. I try to greet people, even those I don't know, cheerfully, with a smile and a positive comment— nothing neutral or negative, and certainly nothing demeaning or sarcastic. I look for those who seem down in their response and take a moment (or more) to be supportive and encouraging. I try to listen at least for a few moments to those whom I can sense need a listener. I never deny someone who says, "Can I ask you a question?" or, "Do you have a minute?" I try to be patient and tolerant even with those who may have an aggressive or hostile attitude. I try to be empathetic always, and to "God bless" others when we part ways. And later, when I'm back home, I consciously try to show my wife and family, as well as friends and neighbors, the goodness and Godliness that I'm confident are within me. I try always to be courteous, pleasant, generous, loving, thoughtful, helpful, thankful, and cooperative. By giving from within myself in these ways, I believe I am manifesting God's characteristics, as best I as a human being can comprehend such. By consciously focusing on bringing good things—Godly things—to others, I feel I am living out God's will for me, and therefore am participating in His Kingdom now, as well as preparing for His Kingdom in eternity.

A powerful, yet simple, description of our Godly duties in the Kingdom of this world was demonstrated to me in the previously referenced retreat given by Rev. Emmanuel Charles McCarthy. In it he put forth the most convincing display of our Christian identity as peacemakers that I've ever encountered. One of the images that he presented was the idea that a person who wishes to make Christ-like changes in the world, need only to perform simple acts of Christ-like work in his day to day life. He said that our little works or words of Christ-like significance are like pebbles tossed onto the calm surface of a morning pond. When that happens, we see the ripples go out, reaching even to the very edges of the pond. Our words, actions, and attitudes that touch maybe just one person in a favorable and God-like way, benefit that person certainly, but then as that person passes his goodness on to someone else, and that person to someone else, and so forth, the original effort that started it all, eventually can have extensive and far reaching effects. So it is clear that when we do even small acts of Christ-like caring, giving, forgiving, and loving, we initiate "ripples" that will positively impact people and situations in such ways that Christ becomes known to others, and God's Kingdom flourishes. So for the Christian, living in the earthly Kingdom of God, it is quite simple. As Fr. McCarthy says, "Love as Christ loved, here and now, and let the ripples go out."

I recall in recent years, a certain Christian youth movement that was promoting Christ by wearing colorful rubberized bracelets embossed with the letters, "W.W.J.D." It stood for "What Would Jesus Do?" and was meant as a reminder of what it takes to live the Christian life. If one considers in each and every situation in his life just how Jesus Himself would have handled it, and responds accordingly, he will truly be following Christ. As I first encountered this "phenomenon" I brushed it off as just a popular, trendy, and probably short-lived way for kids to express a newfound inspiration in their lives. And maybe it was—but maybe it wasn't! The more I thought about this catchy query, the more I couldn't deny that it really is at the center of how all Christians are called to live. To follow Christ is to imitate Christ at all times and in all situations. Once we discover who Jesus is, through the only source of Jesus information available to us, the Christian Scriptures (the New Testament), then imitating Him must become our way of life. As we come to recognize and imitate Jesus as the Son of God, we also recognize God as Father, and as Holy Spirit, and thereby find ourselves living in God's Kingdom here on Earth, as well as preparing for His eternal heavenly Kingdom.

By making these kinds of behaviors and thinking our habits for daily living, we can experience the strength and movement of God in our midst, and we can feel confident, secure, and joyful that God exists with us, and in us, and that we are cooperating with His plans for us. This is what is meant by living in His Kingdom now.

The Sacramental Life

In addition to the work of God's will for us, how else can we stay connected with God as we seek His Kingdom in this world? As Catholic Christians, we need to sincerely pursue a deep and enduring dedication to the sacraments. Participation in the sacramental opportunities of the Church can allow us to live in the Kingdom on Earth, as well as to confidently prepare ourselves for the heavenly Kingdom to come. Each sacrament carries the power to make real what it symbolizes, and thereby derives its significance in our earthly lives. Our faith convinces us that the sacraments actually bring the Godly realm of Heaven into the Godly realm of Earth.

There are seven sacraments in the Catholic Church: the initiating sacraments of Baptism, Eucharist, and Confirmation; the healing sacraments of Reconciliation and Sickness; and the service sacraments of Matrimony and Holy Orders. Each one was established by Christ during His earthly life, and has scriptural evidence to support its reality.

In the sacrament of Baptism, we are both cleansed, and initiated. We are cleansed of all sin, be it "original sin," as committed by the free choice of the first man and woman, our first "parents," Adam and Eve, and then passed down to all subsequent generations of mankind, or be it "actual sins," meaning the offenses against God that we ourselves have chosen to commit. Being thus freed of all sin, we are initiated, or brought into, the ways of Jesus Christ, which offers us eventual eternal salvation in God's heavenly Kingdom. The contingency, of course, is that we live our lives in accordance with the one who's life we were baptized into, namely Jesus Christ. If we carry out our responsibilities as detailed in the Christian Scriptures, and if we fulfill God's expectations for us, as best we as individuals can decipher them to be, then we are accepting God's Kingdom work here in this world, and are preparing to eventually be rewarded in His heavenly Kingdom eternally. Once we have been baptized in the name of Jesus Christ we have been totally immersed, every part of our being, in His ways. The Greek word "baptism" actually means "immersion." Being immersed, and committed to Jesus Christ, we can get up each morning, and live each day, and decide each decision based on that baptism. In doing so, we are living in the Kingdom. Every moment, regardless of the situation, no matter how seemingly negative or positive, big or small, is subjected to the awareness that we are surrounded by and immersed in, the mystery and presence of God. We are immersed in holiness! We are truly living in His Kingdom.

If we have received the Eucharistic host (Holy Communion) in earnest, then we have admitted that we have faith and confidence in who Jesus Christ was and is and will be. The Second Vatican Council (1962-1965) proclaimed the sacrament of Eucharist as being "the source and summit of the Christian life." To us as Catholic Christians, there is nothing more basic and nurturing, and nothing more important to advancing our lives in Godly ways than Eucharist. The Council reminds us that the Eucharist "actually is Jesus Christ — body, blood, soul, and divinity." If we sincerely believe that this man who came into the world over two thousand years ago and lived on this earth, and proclaimed God as "Our Father," and God as love and mercy, and who died a hideous but redemptive death, and was raised from the dead, thus being recognized as the long awaited Messiah and Savior, and if we sincerely believe that we can "see" God through the teachings and the person of Jesus Christ, then God is available to us right now, today. In the Eucharist, we have the memory of Jesus' redemptive sacrifice; we have the consecration, literally meaning the setting aside of bread and wine as being holy; and we have the transubstantiation, literally meaning the changing of one substance (bread and wine) into another (the body and blood of Jesus). Thus, we can believe and we can say that in the sacrament of Eucharist, we have the "real presence" of Jesus Christ, right here physically and spiritually with us, and even *in* us. Our King is here in our presence, and we in His presence. We are living in His realm; we are living in the Kingdom of God.

God's Kingdom here on Earth is encountered and experienced in direct proportion to our involvement in the aspects of holiness that are available to us right here and now. As we participate in the characteristics of God, as revealed by Jesus Christ, we will be experiencing His Kingdom on Earth. Consider mercy as God's most all inclusive characteristic. Mercy is God's absolute will. Mercy is also His absolute willingness to love us and to forgive those of us transgressors who are of repentant heart. He provides us with good things always despite our downfalls and human inadequacies, only because we are His people, His creations, and His own. As human beings, we know ourselves to be imperfect. We are all sinners. We all, sooner or later, transgress

God's will for us. Even those who are most diligently devoted to the service of God in this world, will at times break communication with, relationship with, or cooperation with God our King. Many both Old and New Testament stories, as well as events throughout the course of human history, point to the obvious sinful tendencies of mankind. When such offenses are committed, those of good conscience come to an awareness of responsibility for the transgression, and will feel guilt. If one's conscience is well formed by the teachings of Christ and His Church, then he will know when he has behaved in such un-Christ-like ways and has offended God. As Catholic Christians we always have the possibility of complete, permanent, and guaranteed forgiveness of our sins, right here and now, during our lifetimes through the healing sacrament of Reconciliation (also known as the sacrament of Penance, and the sacrament of Confession). In this sacrament, we don't just communicate with God in prayer and hope to be forgiven. Rather we speak our sins to the priest who sacramentally stands in the place of the person of Christ, and he transmits God's forgiveness and absolution. We are told in the New Testament that Jesus gave His apostles, and thereby our priests as successors to the apostles, the power to forgive sins when He said,

"[Whose sins] you bind on earth shall be bound in heaven, and [whose sins] you loose on earth shall be loosed in heaven." (Matthew 18:18).

Thus, in the mystery of this sacrament, our sins really can be divinely wiped out, divinely forgiven and forgotten...forever!

Ironically, sin in all its ugliness, repulsiveness, and negativity, can be experienced by the Catholic Christian, as an opportunity to refocus on God by merit of his falling away from Him. In falling, we feel a detachment from God since, when in sin, we are missing the intense and intimate presence of God in our lives. By true repentance, in the sacrament of Reconciliation, we experience the joy of God's forgiveness, and we return to the presence of God with an even greater commitment to avoid sin, to remain in His presence, and to remain in His Kingdom way of life. The grace of this sacrament supplies us with the Godly strength, the holy power, that makes it possible for us, as our prayer of contrition says "to avoid the near occasions of sin" (see "Resources" - B.8). What joyful hope, that we might become sinless again, just like when we were baptized, and thereby know that we are even more pleasing to God our King; that we are even more like Jesus Christ; that we are holy; that we are, even if just for a short time, almost perfect, almost like God Himself. Here again, we can see the heavenly Kingdom mingling with the earthly Kingdom. By experiencing the unconditional and boundless mercy and love of God, we can know that we are living in His Kingdom right now.

The real presence of the Holy Spirit is bestowed on the Christian person in the sacrament of Confirmation. It allows the fledgling Christian to become powerful in his faith and powerful in carrying out his evangelistic duties. The sacrament of Baptism initiated and immersed us into the life of Christ. As we gradually come to believe more certainly that Jesus is our savior, the need to spread this belief and awareness to others becomes more apparent, and also becomes imperative. We cannot possess true faith, and expect not to share it. In the sacrament of Confirmation, with the indwelling of the Holy Spirit, Jesus commissions all Christians just as He commissioned His apostles when He said,

"Go therefore and make disciples of all nations…teaching them to observe all that I have commanded you. And behold I am with you always." (Matthew 28:19-20).

Just as Jesus, after His ascension into Heaven, sent the Holy Spirit to His disciples, and the disciples became as if on fire with the energy to spread the faith, and they traveled near and far to tell the good news of the Messiah's arrival and His saving work, so too we as Christ followers, by merit of our Baptism and Confirmation, have that same obligation to go out into the world and spread the good news of our faith to others. To the individual who receives the sacrament of Confirmation sincerely, it will serve as a life long fountain of the spiritual strength necessary for him to witness to others in ways that will ultimately result in the eternal salvation of his soul, as well as the souls of others. It is critically important, of course, for the Christian who has this fountain of strength within him by merit of this sacrament, to "drink" from that fountain frequently. We imbibe and magnify our spiritual strength as we indulge in Eucharist, Reconciliation, Mass, prayer, and repetitive daily efforts to live our lives as the example of Jesus Christ directs us.

The sacraments of Matrimony and Holy Orders are both considered sacraments of service. As such, their differences are few and their similarities are many. The differences are obvious in that married individuals commit themselves to the service of each other and their families, while priests commit themselves to the service of God's family. The similarities include the fact that in both sacraments, covenant commitments are made for the promotion of holy purposes — that is, God's plans. Both sacraments require personal life long, dedication and sacrifice in order to be carried out in the intended fullness. Each one assures the provision of grace (divine power) in return for the faithful carrying out of the commitment. Each one, by merit of the intimate in-volvement in God's plans and purposes, allows those so involved and committed, to live now in His earthly Kingdom.

Our bodies are gloriously made and wonderfully complex but they are also mortal and thereby incapable of enduring long in this earthly realm. Sooner or later we all encounter sickness and death. The Catholic Church is able to transmit God's power and strength to those who are ill, by means of the healing which occurs in the Sacrament of the Sick. The grace of this sacrament allows those who are ill or nearing death, to experience the hope for a holy transition either back to an improved state of health, or on to physical death and the transformation to eternal life. The grace of this sacrament also allows the individual to accept his rightful role as a true servant of God, one who is totally reliant, through His covenant with us, His people, on His plans and on His will. As with the other sacraments we can see how by becoming identified with Godly purposes and by assuming our proper relationship with God, we can come into the assurance through faith that we are at this very moment, even in our sickness or dying, living in His presence, living in His Kingdom.

Sacramental living elevates our minds and hearts, and provides the graces to live in Godly ways. In such living we have the distinct awareness that we are truly living in His Kingdom.

The Liturgical Life

In addition to the sacraments, we as Catholics also have the Mass and the liturgical calendar to keep us focused on those parts of God's Kingdom that exist here on Earth, as well as in Heaven.

The Mass, of course, is the Church's highest and most important form of prayer. In the Mass, God's people are nourished by His words from both the Old and the New Testaments and also, and most importantly, by the reception of Holy Communion (the Eucharist) which is the real body and blood of Jesus Christ. His people physically come together in Churches all over the world on the Christian Sabbath day each Sunday, and on special Holy Days, to praise and to worship Him. We can experience a certain portion of the heavenly Kingdom through the prayers, the Word, and the Eucharist. To the extent that we seriously and sincerely participate in the Mass, we reap the holy rewards of peace, mercy, security, and comfort. Our participation requires our best efforts to concentrate and stay focused on what's really going on at Mass. We have come both to be nourished by the Word and Eucharist, as well as to give praise, honor, glory, and thanksgiving to God in three persons, the Holy Trinity. We need to say the prayers thoughtfully, join in the responses, sing the hymns, listen attentively to the priest's homily, wish each other the peace of Christ joyfully, receive Holy Communion fervently, and make sure to spend time after receiving to thank God for providing our salvation through the works and ongoing presence of Jesus Christ. We are then sent back out into the world, when our priest says, "Go in peace to love and serve the Lord." In the days of the Latin Mass, the priest would conclude with the words, "Ite, missa est," meaning, "Go, you are dismissed," or said another way, "Go, you are sent." Interestingly, and not by accident, the word "Mass" is actually derived from the Latin word "missa," meaning "send," and refers to the concept of our prayer being completed and so we are being dismissed, or sent out. After coming in and being duly sated with the nourishing Word and Eucharist, we are ready to be sent back out into the world with the intent of bringing the awareness of God's presence, love, and Kingship to others. And when the days of the week are over, and we are in some sense depleted of the spiritual energy provided by the Mass, we dutifully return to Mass the next

Sunday to again be nourished, strengthened, and revitalized, only to be sent out again for Godly purposes. To the Catholic Christian who is cognizant of this process, Sunday Mass becomes truly the high point of his week. Why shouldn't he relish the powerfully energizing meal designed and provided by the King Himself, for the purpose of serving Him by doing His glorious and necessary work?

The Liturgical calendar guides us through the events and testimonies of the Christian scriptures. The calendar starts with the first Sunday of Advent, usually in late November or early December. The word "advent" means "before the coming," referring to the time before the coming of Christ into the world in the person of Jesus of Nazareth, which we celebrate on Christmas day. There are four weeks of Advent preparation. These four weeks symbolize the approximately 4,000 years of anticipation and preparation that the Jewish people experienced before the Messiah's arrival. The Hebrew word "Messiah" means "the anointed one," as does the Greek word "Christus" from which we derive "Christ."

This title refers to the One who was foretold in the Hebrew scriptures (the Old Testament), as being specially chosen by God to come into the world at some point in history to bring peace to the world and to save His people. Those who came to accept the teachings, leadership, and charisma of Jesus, recognizing Him as that One, the "Holy One of God" (John 7:69), the anointed One, became known as Christians. During the Christmas season (i.e. the weeks following Christmas day) the Church continues to remind us of God's gift of the Messiah.

After a season of "Ordinary" time, referring to the ordinal numbers used to count the Sundays, we arrive at the season of Lent. The word "lent" is derived from an Old English word, "lengten," meaning the season of "the lengthening of days," referring to the late winter time when daylight hours are increasing, eventually leading to Easter Sunday. The Lenten season is initiated with Ash Wednesday. On this day, we are blessed with ashes and reminded of our lowly, fragile, and temporary nature as human beings, and also of God's will and desire for us to spend eternity with Him in the heavenly Kingdom. Then we experience forty days (six and a half weeks excluding Sundays) of special prayer, sacrifice, almsgiving, and charitable works. This corresponds to the forty days Jesus spent in the desert, prior to initiating His ministry. It prepares us to focus on the three days (the Triduum) that include Jesus' last supper with His apostles, His suffering and death, and His resurrection from the dead on Easter Sunday. The word "Easter" is derived from the Old English word "Eastre" meaning "Spring." Easter Sunday falls on the first Sunday after the first full moon of Spring. Then there are fifty days of the Easter season, rejoicing in the work of our salvation that has been accomplished by Jesus Christ, and recognized by all Christians. This culminates on Pentecost Sunday. The word "Pentecost" refers to the fifty days after Jesus' resurrection, at which time, after ascending to His Father in Heaven in His glorified bodily form, He gifted His disciples with the Holy Spirit (literally the

"Godly breath"). The Holy Spirit for them, and to this day for all Christians and people of Godly pursuits and intents, provides the desire, motivation, character, strength, power, and stamina to bring the meaning of Jesus' life and work, and the real possibility of eternal and heavenly salvation, to others in this world.

After Easter and the Easter season, the most joyous time of the Christian calendar year, we resume Ordinary time, and the counting of Sundays until we arrive at the end of the liturgical year on Christ the King Sunday, reminding us of His supremacy in our lives. The very next Sunday begins a new liturgical year with the first Sunday of Advent.

Each liturgical year is labeled "A," "B," or "C," to designate the predominant source of the gospel readings that are occurring at Sunday Masses during that year. Cycle A consists predominantly of readings from St. Matthew, cycle B from St. Mark, and cycle C from St. Luke. St. John's gospels are placed strategically throughout all three cycles. Thus, the Catholic who is dutifully attending Mass each Sunday will be listening to a wide array of gospel verses and teachings over every three year period, allowing him to become very well acquainted with the teachings of Jesus Christ, as revealed by the writing of the four Evangelists. This ongoing diligent participation in the scriptures, and the life and activities of His Church, brings us as serious Catholic Christians to a familiarity and closeness to Jesus our Redeemer, that graces us and strengthens us to embrace God's will for us in this world. As we do so, we clearly come to realize that even as we are living our mortal lives, we are truly living in His Kingdom.

The Personal Prayer Life

We also maintain closeness to God our King through our personal prayer lives. Whether verbal or non-verbal, prayer is essentially speaking to God from the heart, that is to say, from our souls, from our spiritual beings. For some serious God seekers, prayer may be a complex or even a formal process, while for others it may be quite simple or informal. Prayer can be done at a specific time of day, such as before bedtime, or upon arising in the morning, or at midday, or at meal times. Prayer can happen in a specific location, such as a particular room in the house, or in a church. Prayer can of course also be done at random times and frequencies, at any time at all, or in any place at all. We can make good use of idle moments by resorting to prayer when waiting in a checkout line, or during an airport delay; while driving in the car, or waiting in the doctor's office. There's no limit to the opportunities for prayer. God is always and everywhere available to our spiritual beings. Regardless of the prayer plans that we adopt, the important thing is to pray often, at least every day, and preferably many times a day. If we are to understand something of who God is and what he desires and expects of us in our earthly lives, we must maintain communication with Him. And just as it's important to communicate often with a friend in order to maintain familiarity, comfort, and confidence in that relationship, so too it's important to maintain communication with God.

I remember once reading a newspaper advice column in which a teenage girl was discussing a particular family problem, and said that her father did not believe in God, but she and her mother did. She mentioned that her mother frequently argued with her father in trying to convince him to believe. She also said that her father frequently expressed the philosophy that he would rather believe there was no God than to believe in a God that didn't answer his prayers. The advice columnist rightly pointed out that belief in God is not something that can be forced on someone. And I would add that if we truly believe in God, then we know that we have been specially blessed and invited by Him to have that secure and ongoing confidence that He is our creator, our reason for existing, and that He really does care for us. In the above scenario I wondered why that father, who apparently at one time had some degree of awareness of God as a supernatural being, had abandoned Him? He seemed to feel that if God was not giving him what he was requesting in his prayers, that that meant God was not responding to him. How did he get the idea that God was there to give him what he wanted and what he asked for? He apparently felt God's role in his life should be to provide him with whatever he wanted, or thought that he needed. Those of us who have faith, clearly understand that we are the ones whose role it is to serve God and to carry out His will. We know that God our King, gives us what we need. What we want or think that we need may or may not be what God knows that we need. God always has a plan for accomplishing our salvation, and that is really all we need.

When we pray with certain requests (prayers of petition), we should always include the words, "if it is Your will." Reflect on Jesus Himself praying in the Garden of Gethsemane on the night before He was crucified,

> "Father, if you are willing, take this cup away from me. Nevertheless, let your will be done, not mine." (Luke 22:42,43).

Even with this most impassioned plea from His only son, did God grant to Jesus, the man, what He prayed for — to be released from the torture, suffering, and death that was to face Him? No! God's will to redeem mankind was to be accomplished. Jesus, the man, resisted His fate. Jesus, the Christ, accepted God's will. If we do so also, we will not be disappointed if such petitions do not materialize as we might wish them to. In fact, we can still be thrilled and amazed, realizing that God's will has thus unfolded and been accomplished, even though it might not have been our wishes. Recall from the Lord's Prayer, how is it that "thy Kingdom" will come? It is by, "thy will" being done.

In our prayer lives we should always have the attitude, no matter what our level of practice or accomplishment is, that there is always room for improvement. We should not let our prayer lives become unchanging, stagnant, or boring. After all, communicating with God our King is the highest privilege we as human beings, and His servants, can have. So, prayers of petition are not the only way we should pray. We should frequently speak to God also to praise and glorify Him and to adore Him. And just as we would thank a friend for giving us a gift or sharing something with us, our prayers of thanksgiving to God should never cease since He has given us so much— in fact, all that we have, and all that we are. And we need to be humble before God—He is our King, we are His servants! We need to admit, and remind ourselves, of our lowliness and our wishes to please Him. We need to invite God into our hearts and minds, and to be humble before Him— He is our King, we are His servants!

Conclusion

The "Conclusion" part of a book, of course, is meant to be just that —the conclusion, the ending. It brings the reader to a point where, having read the book's contents, he is looking forward to the author's final thoughts and parting comments. When I myself get to this point of a book, I find myself making a judgment as to how worthwhile the book was, or wasn't, meaning how did I relate to its contents, how much significance did it have for me, how inspirational was it, or how can I use the information presented to make my life better.

And so, I hope that you, the reader, indeed have discovered some angle about living your own life that will enrich and enliven you on into the future.

The one most important concept I had hoped to express in this book, and convey to the reader, is that the Kingdom of God, the realm of God, exists not only in the eternal Kingdom of Heaven in the hereafter, but also wherever and however the work of God is manifested, even in this very tangible, here and now, earthly setting. If there's awareness of God's work in Heaven, and if there's awareness of God's work here on Earth, then the Kingdom of God really is a continuum of His presence — both in Heaven and on Earth! It only makes sense to think of all existence as His Kingdom, that is, "heaven and earth," and "the seen and the unseen." And how exciting and fulfilling it is to awaken each morning and realize that God the King is still right here, and right now. We get to live another day in His earthly Kingdom, preparing for another day when we hope to be transformed to live in His heavenly Kingdom eternally. And our duty this day is the same as it is every day of our lives: to thank God for our faith in Him; to be open to whatever His will might be for us; and to carry out His will in Christ-like ways to the best of our capabilities. To recognize God as our King and to serve Him here and now is to live in the Kingdom of God.

Finally, and hopefully to urge you on in holy ways, I offer you this thought. If we are people of sincere faith, convinced that God is our King and our only reason for being, then we will realize that our search for Him, that is, our search to know Him, to love Him, and to serve Him during this life time will never cease until we exhale our final breath. We must continually push on toward understanding and serving Him as best we can. By living as such, we can come to say with St. Paul,

"Brothers and sisters…just one thing: forgetting what lies behind, straining forward to what lies ahead, I continue my pursuit toward the goal, the prize of God's upward calling in Jesus Christ." (Philippians 3:13-14).

Resources

A. Books

1. Abba! Father!, Gerald Mahoney, Crossroad Publishing Co., 1982
2. August 9, Emmanuel Charles McCarthy
3. Bread Broken and Shared, Paul Bernier, Ave Maria Press, 1981
4. Behold the Cross, Toney Kelly, CSR, Liguori Publications, 1999
5. Called to Holiness, Ralph Martin, Ignatius Press, 1970
6. Catechism of the Catholic Church, St Paul Books and Media, 1994
7. Crossing the Threshold of Hope, Pope John Paul II, Alfred A. Knopf, 1994
8. Exploring the Identity and Mission of Jesus, John Michael Perry, Sheed and Ward, 1996
9. Exploring the Resurrection of Jesus, John Michael Perry, Sheed and Ward, 1993
10. Handbook for Spiritual Growth, Phillip St. Romaine, Liguori Publications, 1986
11. Here on the Way to There, William H. Shannon, St Anthony Messenger Press, 2005
12. If Your Mind Wanders at Mass, Thomas Howard, Franciscan University Press, 1994
13. Inspired-The Breath of God, Jeanna Laufer and Kenneth S. Levins, Doubleday Press, 1998
14. Jesus and His Message, Leo Mahon, ACTA Publications, 2000
15. Jesus of the Gospels, Arthur E. Zannoni, St. Anthony Press, 1996
16. Jesus the Jewish Theologian, Brad H. Young, Hendrickson Publications, 1999
17. Jesus the Christ, Thomas G. Welnandy, OFM, Our Sunday Visitor Publishing, 2003

18. Last Things First, Regis J. Flaherty, Our Sunday Visitor Publishing, 1997
19. Living the Beatitudes Today, Bill Dodds and Michael Dodds, O.P., Loyola Press, 1997
20. Living the Mysteries, Scott Hahn and Mike Aquilina, Our Sunday Visitor Publishing, 2003
21. Living the Catholic Faith, Charles J. Chaput, OFM, Servant Publications, 2001
22. Living Peace, John Dear, Doubleday Press, 2001
23. Lord Have Mercy, Scott Hahn, Doubleday Press, 2003
24. Meeting Jesus Again for the First Time, Marcus J. Borg, Harper Collins Publishers, 1995
25. On Being Catholic, Thomas Howard, Ignatius Press, 1997
26. Rediscovering Catholicism, Matthew Kelly, Beacon Publishing Co., 2002
27. Rise, Let Us Be on Our Way, Pope John Paul, II, Warren Brothers, 2004
28. Rome Sweet Home, Scott Hahn, Ignatius Press
29. Seeking Jesus in the Old Testament, Renu Rita Silvano, Our Sunday Visitor Publishing Company, 2008
30. Swear To God, Scott Hahn, Doubleday Press, 2004
31. The Fathers of the Church, Mike Aquilina, Our Sunday Visitor Publishing Co., 1999
32. The Heart of Loving, Eugene Kennedy, Argus Communications, 1973
33. The Joy of Following Jesus, J. Oswald Sanders, Moody Press, 1994
34. The Kingdom Within, John A. Sanford, Paulist Press, 1970
35. The Knowledge of the Holy, A.W. Tozer, Harper One, 1978
36. The Lamb's Supper, Scott Hahn, Doubleday Press
37. The Meaning of Success, Michel Quoist, Fides Publishers, 1966
38. The New American BIBLE, St Joseph Edition, Benziger Publishing Co, 1991
39. The Ten Commandments, Mitch Finley, Liguori Press, 2000
40. The Truth of Catholicism, George Weigel, Harper Collins Publishers, 2002
41. Through Moses to Jesus, Carlo M. Martini, S J., Ave Maria Press, *1988*
42. To Know Christ Jesus, Frank Sheed, Ignatius Press, 1980
43. What is a Jew?, Rabbi Morris Kertzer, Simon and Schuster, 1996
44. Who is Christ, Anthony Padovano, Ave Maria Press, 1967
45. Why Am I Afraid to Love?, John Powell, S.J, Argus Communication, 1972
46. Why Am I afraid to Tell You Who I am?, John Powell, SJ, Argus Communication, 1969
47. Words Made Flesh, Fran Ferder, Ave Maria Press, 1990

B. Prayers

1. The Prayer of St Francis of Assisi
   Lord, make me an instrument of thy peace.
   where there is hatred let me sow love;
   where there is injury, pardon;
   where there is doubt, faith;
   where there is despair, hope;
   where there is darkness, light;
   and where there is sadness, joy.

   O, Divine Master, grant that I may not so much seek
   to be consoled, as to console;
   to be understood, as to understand;
   to be loved, as to love.

   For, it is in giving that we receive,
   in pardoning that we are pardoned,
   and in dying that we are born into eternal life. Amen.

2. The Prayer of St. Ignatius Loyola
   Dearest Lord, Teach me to be generous,
   teach me to serve You as You deserve —
   to give and not to count the cost,
   to fight and not to heed the wounds,
   to toil and not to seek for rest,
   to labor and not to ask for reward,
   save that of knowing I am doing Your will. Amen.

3. The Prayer of St Michael the Archangel
   St. Michael the Archangel, defend us in battle;
   be our protection against the wickedness and snares of the devil.
   Rebuke him O God we humbly beseech thee,
   and do thou O Prince of the heavenly host,
   by thy divine power,
   thrust into hell Satan and all the evil spirits
   who roam through the world
   seeking the ruin of souls. Amen.

4. Hail, Holy Queen
   Hail, Holy Queen, Mother of Mercy,
   Our life, our sweetness, and our hope.
   To thee do we cry, poor banished children of Eve.
   To thee do we send up our sighs,
   mourning and weeping in this valley of tears.

Turn then, most gracious advocate, thine eyes of mercy toward us, and after this our exile, show unto us the blessed fruit of thy womb, Jesus.
O clement, O loving, O sweet Virgin Mary.
Pray for us O holy Mother of God,
That we may be made worthy of the promises of Christ. Amen.

5. Memorare
Remember, O most gracious Virgin Mary,
That never was it known that anyone who fled to thy protection,
Implored thy help, or sought thy intercession, was left unaided.
Inspired with this confidence, I fly unto thee, O virgin of virgins my mother.
To thee do I come, before thee I stand, sinful and sorrowful.
O Mother of the Word Incarnate, despise not my petitions,
But in thy mercy hear and answer me. Amen.

6. Hail Mary
Hail Mary, full of grace, the Lord is with thee.
Blessed art though amongst women,
And blessed is the fruit of thy womb, Jesus.
Holy Mary, Mother of God, pray for us sinners,
Now, and at the hour of our death. Amen.

7. The Lord's Prayer
Our Father, who art in Heaven, hallowed be thy name.
Thy Kingdom come. Thy will be done, on Earth as it is in Heaven.
Give us this day our daily bread, and forgive us our trespasses
As we forgive those who trespass against us.
And lead us not into temptation, but deliver us from evil. Amen.

8. Act of Contrition
O my God, I am heartily sorry for having offended thee.
And I detest all my sins because of thy just punishment,
but most of all because they offend thee, my God,
who art all good and deserving of all my love.
I firmly resolve with the help of thy grace, to sin no more,
and to avoid the near occasions of sin. Amen.

9. Easter Antiphon
Christians, to the Paschal victim offer your thankful praises.
A lamb the sheep redeemeth.
Christ who only is sinless reconciles sinners to the Father.
Death and life have contended in that combat stupendous.

The Prince of Life, who died, reigns immortal.
Speak, Mary, declaring what thou sawest wayfaring.
"The tomb of Christ who is risen. The glory of Jesus'
Resurrection.
Bright angels attesting. The shroud and napkin resting.
Yea, Christ my hope is risen. To Galilee He goes before thee."
Christ indeed from death has risen, our new life obtaining.
Have mercy victor King, ever reigning. Amen. Alleluia.

10. One More Day
Thank you Lord for watching over us.
Through our task, You make us victorious.
We praise Your name, most great and glorious.
Thank you Lord, for one more day.

11. The Jesus Prayer
Lord Jesus Christ, Son of God, Have mercy on me, a sinner.

12. The Apostle's Creed
I believe in God, the Father Almighty,
  Creator of Heaven and Earth
  [or as is said in the Nicene Creed: "of all that is seen and unseen"]
And in Jesus Christ, His only Son, our Lord,
  Who was conceived by the Holy Spirit, born of the Virgin Mary,
Suffered under Pontius Pilate, was crucified, died, and was buried.
He descended into Hell.
The third day He rose again from the dead.
  He ascended into Heaven, and sits at the right hand of God, the
Father Almighty, from thence He shall come to judge the living and
the dead.
  I believe in the Holy Spirit, the holy catholic church, the
communion of saints, the forgiveness of sins, the resurrection of the
body, and life everlasting. Amen.

13. Aspiration
Lord, I am not worthy to receive You, but only say the word and I
shall be healed.

14. Aspiration.
Jesus, meek and humble of heart, make my heart like unto thine.

C. *Biblical Verses*

1. Numbers 6:22-27 (Blessing of the Israelites)
The Lord bless you and keep you!

The Lord let His face shine upon you, and be gracious to you!
The Lord look upon you kindly, and give you peace!

2. 23rd Psalm
The Lord is my shepherd, I shall not want.
In verdant pastures He gives me repose, beside restful waters He leads me.
He refreshes my soul.
He guides me in right paths for His name's sake.
Even though I walk in the dark valley, I fear no evil,
For You are at my side with Your rod and Your staff that give me courage.
You spread the table before me in the sight of my foes.
You anoint my head with oil.
My cup overflows.
Only goodness and kindness shall follow me all the days of my life,
and I will live in the House of the Lord for years to come.

3. Matthew 5:3-12 (The Beatitudes)
Blessed are the poor in spirit, for theirs is the Kingdom of Heaven.
Blessed are they who mourn, for they will be comforted.
Blessed are the meek, for they will inherit the land.
Blessed are they who hunger and thirst for righteousness, for they will be satisfied.
Blessed are the merciful, for they will be shown mercy.
Blessed are the clean of heart, for they will see God.
Blessed are the peacemakers, for they will be called children of God.
Blessed are they who are persecuted for the sake of righteousness,
  for theirs is the Kingdom of Heaven.
Blessed are you when they insult you and persecute you and utter
every kind of evil against you falsely because of me.
  Rejoice and be glad for your reward will be great in Heaven.
  Thus they persecuted the prophets who were before you.

4. Matthew 28:21-22
Then Peter approaching asked Him, "Lord if my brother sins against me, how often must I forgive him? As many as seven times?" Jesus answered, "I say to you, not seven times, but seventy-seven times.

5. I Corinthians 13:1-13
If I speak in human and angelic tongues, but do not have love,
  I am a resounding gong or a clashing cymbal.

And if I have the gift of prophecy, and comprehend all mysteries and all knowledge; if I have all faith so as to move mountains, but do not have love,

I am nothing.

If I give away everything I own, and if I hand my body over so that I may boast, but do not have love,

I gain nothing.

Love is patient, love is kind. It is not jealous, it is not pompous, it is not inflated, it is not rude, it is not quick-tempered, it does not brood over injury, it does not seek its own interests, it is not quick-tempered, it does not rejoice over wrongdoing but rejoices with the truth.

Love bears all things, believes all things, hopes all things, endures all things.

Love never fails.

If there are prophecies, they will be brought to nothing;

if tongues, they will cease;

if knowledge, it will be brought to nothing.

For we know partially and we prophesy partially,

but when the perfect comes, the partial will pass away.

When I was a child, I used to talk as a child, think as a child, reason as a child. When I became a man, I put aside childish things. At present we see indistinctly, as in a mirror, but then face to face.

At present I know partially; then I shall know fully, as I am fully known.

So faith, hope, and love remain, these three;

But the greatest of these is love.